AS THE TREE CHANGES

BROOKE GILLIAM

CONTENTS

For

My loving husband and wild child

INTRODUCTION

There is something sacred in the way a tree survives: how it stands through storms, loses what it can no longer carry, and still finds the courage to bloom again. A tree survives not by staying the same, but by changing. By surrendering its leaves, by reaching for light during the hardest winters, by trusting that new growth will come even after the coldest nights. Trees do not rush their healing, nor do they apologize for the seasons they must endure. They simply move through them. And in my own life, I've learned that I must do the same.

This book is, at its core, a record of those seasons.

The poems that follow trace a cycle of breaking, reaching, becoming, and releasing—each one echoing the quiet wisdom of a tree's life. I chose the tree's cycle as the guiding metaphor because it captures the truth of healing more honestly than any straight line ever could. Healing is not linear; it is seasonal. It returns to us in stages, soft at times, brutal at others, but always transformative. And just when we think we've reached the end of one phase, something shifts, and a new season begins.

This collection is divided into four sections, each one shaped by a stage in a tree's natural rhythm. Together, they form the emotional journey of a life lived honestly, painfully, joyfully, and with the hope that new growth is always possible.

I. Bare Branches

The first section, *Bare Branches*, holds poems from the darkest months of my life. It includes moments of trauma, depression, anxiety, and the kind of loneliness that settles deep in the bones. A tree stripped of its leaves stands exposed, every limb visible, every flaw illuminated by the harshest light. That is what these poems are: unadorned truth—the part of healing that often goes unseen, yet forms the foundation for everything that follows. Writing them was an act of standing still in the dark and admitting, *This is where I am.*

II. Seeking Light

The second section, *Seeking Light*, holds poems from the tender days of becoming, when hope begins to stir through the cracks. These are the moments of reaching, of learning how to trust the warmth again. The poems here explore love, longing, and desire, but also the quiet persistence of a heart that refuses to stop searching for connection. They are fragile, luminous things, carrying the ache of wanting and the sweetness of beginnings

III. Verdant Canopy

The third section, *Verdant Canopy*, is where life grows dense and abundant. It is a season of parenting, joy, family, sacrifice, responsibility, and the storms that shake the branches but never reach the roots. This is a season of fullness: of carrying weight, of nurturing others, of standing tall even when the sky darkens. Here, I write about what it means to hold and to be held, to offer shelter even when I am weathered myself. A blooming tree is beautiful, yes, but it is also strong, worn, useful, and alive in every direction.

IV. Falling Leaves

The final section, *Falling Leaves*, is the season of release. Healing, in truth, often looks less like blooming and more like letting go. Letting go of pain, of old versions of ourselves, of the weight we carried through earlier seasons. In these poems, leaves fall not in defeat, but in liberation. Here, I write about self-love, forgiveness, resilience, and the quiet courage of choosing lightness after long-held heaviness.

***

This tree cycle matters to me because these poems are not just art; they are evidence of survival. Every season represented here is one I have lived through—moments when I broke, moments when I reached, moments when I bloomed, and moments when I had to release what hurt. A tree does not explain its seasons; it simply lives them. I wanted to give myself permission to do the same.

The metaphor reminds me that nothing stays frozen forever, that no wound is final, and that every shedding makes space for something new. Most importantly, it honors the truth that growth does not mean perfection; it means perseverance. It means staying rooted even when everything changes.

This book is my way of offering that truth to anyone who needs it.

It is a reminder that—

Your bare branches are not the end.
Your seeking light is proof you are still growing.
Your verdant canopy is worthy, even if it's wild.
Your falling leaves are not a failure;
they are a release.
And through every season, you remain whole.

BARE BRANCHES

The Quiet One

She was the quiet one. Everyone said it like it was a compliment. So polite. So well-behaved. So easy. She didn't throw tantrums or demand attention. She knew better. She'd learned how to fold herself up small enough to fit the spaces adults left behind. Once, when she was about four, she sat cross-legged on the carpet in her pink Barbie nightgown while the grown-ups talked around her. Loud voices. Glasses clinking. Cigarette smoke curling into the air. She was sitting near the couch, near the noise, but not part of it. At first, she waited for someone to notice her. To scoop her up and say it was late, that she should be in bed. But no one did. Minutes passed. Then hours. Her legs tingled, went numb beneath her. Her head ached from holding in too many thoughts. No one looked down. No one asked if she was okay. So she stared at a spot on the wall and tried to make her mind float away from her body. She told herself to stay quiet. To stay still. That was what made them proud. That was what kept things peaceful.

They said she was such a good girl. But inside, she was unraveling. Not loud and dramatic. No, her unraveling was slow and silent, like threads slipping loose from a hem. She didn't have the words for what she was feeling. She just knew something was wrong with her that no one else seemed to see. That her chest felt too tight sometimes, like her ribs were a birdcage for something too wild to name. She thought if she tried harder, was better, was quieter, maybe the ache inside her would go away. But it didn't.

It grew.

It grew while they praised her for being easy. It grew in all the moments she wanted to cry but smiled instead. It grew in the silence they mistook for peace. And it followed her into every room she entered for years—this feeling that she was too much and never enough at the same time.

They never remembered that night. But she did. She remembered the Barbie nightgown. The sharp sting of carpet on her knees. The way the voices never once said her name.

The Man in the House

She never called him Dad.
He wasn't.
He was rage in skin.
He was slamming doors,
breaking silence
like it owed him something.

He had a face
that curled around insults
like smoke.
Eyes that looked for weakness
like it was a game.
She never knew what would set him off—
a glass left on the counter,
a look held too long,
nothing at all.

The air would thicken
before the storm.
A breath too loud,
a step too quick,
and he would rise—
voice cracking through the walls,
fists clenched around nothing
but heat.

She learned stillness.
She learned how to disappear
without leaving the room.
She learned how to keep
her breath shallow,
her gaze down,
her heart tucked somewhere
he couldn't reach.

He never struck her.
But the house
still remembers
how she shook.

The Flicker

It starts without warning. A flicker, a shift, like the room tilts half an inch and I'm the only one who feels it. My skin goes tight. My stomach drops. Something is wrong. I don't know what, but it's coming. It's always coming. Anxiety doesn't announce itself gently. It grabs me by the spine and whispers, *you're not safe*. It doesn't need a reason. It just is.

I feel like I'm standing in the middle of the street naked, and everyone can see me. Every thought, every flaw, every crack in my mask. I feel watched even when I'm alone. I feel cracked open. Exposed. I can't breathe right, can't move right, can't think in straight lines. My chest feels like it might cave in, like there's a weight pressing down on it but nothing's there. Nothing anyone else can see anyway.

Every sound is sharper. Every glance feels like a threat. I am on high alert for something I can't name. It's not a panic attack yet. But it's close. It's buzzing just beneath my skin. I don't know what to do with my hands. I don't know where to look. I keep swallowing nothing. My throat is dry. My heart keeps skipping beats like it's trying to outrun whatever's chasing me. But there's nothing there. There's never anything there.

But my body doesn't believe me. My body believes it's the end. That something terrible is about to happen. That I won't survive this one. That I'll shatter in public or collapse in private or finally scream loud enough for everyone to hear how broken I am.

And the worst part? No one knows. No one sees. I still look normal. I still smile. I still nod. Because anxiety doesn't care about what's real. It just needs me to feel like I'm drowning while everyone else is breathing fine.

The Background Friend

High school hallways felt
like runways for girls
who knew how to shine.
I wasn't one of them.
I wasn't ugly,
but I wasn't magnetic either.
I was the girl walking slightly behind,
nodding along,
laughing on cue,
just grateful to be invited.

I had friends,
but not the kind
who stayed up texting me at midnight,
not the kind who saved me a seat,
who told me secrets
without looking both ways first.
I was filler.
Extra.
Always the second choice,
or third.
Never the best anything to anyone.

I didn't want to go to parties.
Didn't care about football games
or flirting in the bleachers.

I wanted to go home,
put on pajamas at six,
and get lost in a book
where someone like me
mattered.

They loved music that pulsed in your chest,
selfies under bathroom lights,
talking over each other until their voices blurred.
I loved silence.
And made-up people
who felt more real
than the ones who forgot
to text me back.

I watched best friends take photos
in matching hoodies,
sign yearbooks
with inside jokes
I was never part of.
And I smiled.
Because it was easier
than saying I felt like a shadow
with no name.

Something in the Dark

In the daytime,
my room is mine.
A fortress of paperbacks and playlists,
walls covered by posters,
blankets kicked to the end of the bed
like I've been too busy living inside a story
to care about making things neat.

I hum with the music,
let words float from page to page,
feel like I belong here:
in this mess,
in this quiet,
in this tiny world with the door shut
and no one asking for anything.

But at night,
the air changes.

I turn off the lamp
but keep the hallway light bleeding in
just enough
to see the edges of things.
I lie still,
staring at the ceiling,
pretending I don't hear

the floorboards sigh.

Sometimes the bed shifts.
Like weight.

I stop breathing then.
Eyes closed, body frozen,
as if stillness
could make me vanish.
As if being silent enough
could keep the dark
from noticing me.

And in the morning,
I play the music louder.
Stack the books higher.
Make the room mine again,
until the sun leaves
and everything
starts over.

Milk-Stained Ghost

I thought it would feel like love.
The kind you see in pictures,
soft light,
quiet smiles,
tiny fingers wrapped around yours
like a promise.

But the first time I looked at him,
I felt
nothing.

Just a stillness
too loud to ignore.
Like my body had broken open
and left the rest of me behind.
Like I was watching a stranger
hold a child
we both didn't know how to love.

I smiled when people visited.
Said, "I'm fine,"
while my mind whispered
drive into the tree
drive into the tree
drive into the goddamn tree.

At night, I'd stare at the door
and wonder how far I could get
before someone noticed I was gone.
Middle of the night
keys in hand
baby sleeping
husband sleeping
heart screaming
just leaverunasfastasyoucan

And then the silence.
Then the guilt.
Then the ache
that settled in my chest
and refused to move out.

Everyone kept saying
"he's beautiful,"
"you're so lucky,"
"so happy for you!"
and I wanted to scream
then why can't I feel it?
why do I want to disappear
more than I want to hold him?

I was supposed to be glowing.
But I was drowning,
quietly,
so no one would hear it
and call me broken.

I still got up.
Changed diapers.
Rocked him in the dark.
I still showed up.

But some days
I was nothing
more
than a ghost
with milk-stained clothes
and eyes too tired
to beg for help.

Anticipation

I was already embarrassed
before they even looked at me,
like my body
had done something wrong
just by being there.

I laughed first,
just in case.
Kept my head down,
shrunk my voice
small enough to ignore.

Their words were sharp,
but it was the waiting
that cut deeper.
The knowing it was coming,
the feeling
that maybe
I deserved it.

Is Anyone There?

Loneliness claws beneath my skin, an ache that won't release its grip. It fills my chest like smoke, thick and choking, until I can barely breathe. I whisper into the quiet just to hear a voice, any voice, but the echo dies before it reaches me. I am reaching out with trembling hands, begging the air to hold me, to remind me I am still here.

maybe it's just me

i overthink
    everything.
    what i said
    what i didn't
    how i looked when i said it.
    how they looked at me.
    did they even notice me?

everyone's doing better than me.
    they move like they belong
    they speak like their voice
    was never something
    they had to earn.

i shrink
    without anyone asking me to.
    too loud?
    too weird?
    too much?
    not enough?

i rewrite texts.
    then delete them.
    then wish i'd sent them.
    then wonder
    why anyone would care

what i have to say
in the first place.

i want to be someone else
    but only on the days
    i can't even look in the mirror
    without thinking
    why are you like this?

everyone is better than me
    &
    i don't know how to stop
    believing it.

Bare and Still

The branches hang heavy beneath unseen rain,
roots clutching the earth in silent pain.
No leaves to catch sunlight, no song in the air.
Just the ache of surviving when nothing feels fair.

SEEKING LIGHT

Broken Mirror

I don't know if I want to see myself clearly.
The thought terrifies me.
What if all I find is damage,
just a pile of mistakes
masquerading as a person?

I avoid mirrors for more than my face.
I avoid the stillness,
the silence,
the moments when the truth might crawl out.

Sometimes I feel like I am made only of survival.
No softness, no joy,
just the reflex of holding my breath
and bracing for the next blow.

If I strip everything down,
what is left?
Do I have anything to offer
besides my brokenness?

I want to believe there's more—
but wanting and believing
are not the same thing.

The World Only Listens to Those Who Shout

I keep offering pieces of myself
in the language I know best.
Silence, softness,
a tilt of the heart.
But the world only listens
to those who shout.

Collective Effervescence

I never used to cry.
People said I was heartless,
that I didn't care about anyone but myself.
I used to laugh it off,
pretending they were wrong,
but maybe I believed them.

It felt safer not to feel too much,
safer to stay dry-eyed at funerals,
to keep still when others shook with joy.
Emotion was something I watched from a distance,
like fireworks through glass.

But now, I cry at parades.
At the swell of a marching band,
the confetti falling like snow,
the strangers cheering in unison.
It undoes me.

I cry at graduations,
when names echo through gymnasiums,
and mothers clutch programs
as if they were newborns.
Something in that joy shatters me open.

Maybe I've softened,

or maybe I've finally cracked.
Now I see how feeling binds us,
how a thousand hearts beating at once
can reach inside mine
and say: you're here, too.

I cry because I finally understand
what it means to belong,
how the world hums with shared emotion,
and I was numb to it for so long.

Funny, isn't it?
The girl who never felt enough
now weeps for everything.
Not from sadness,
but from being alive in it all.

Light Through the Cracks

It starts small. Like a crack in the dark I'd built around myself. The air moves differently, almost tender, as if the world itself takes a breath beside me. Then it happens. A smile. Simple. Unplanned. It catches me off guard, blooming from somewhere I thought was gone. For a moment, I forget the weight of my own mind. Light gathers in the corners, spilling quietly through the cracks, and I feel something I can't name. Something like joy, raw and fragile, but real. It hums in my chest, this soft reminder that maybe I am not beyond saving. Maybe the ache was never meant to be endless. Maybe the smallest warmth is all it takes for the frost to begin to melt.

Elsewhere

I slip between pages
and flee—
to lands thick with magic,
where dragons breathe warmth
instead of fear,
where dystopian towns burn
but somehow still bloom.

Here, I'm not quiet.

Here, I fight.

Here, I fly.

And when the world gets too loud—
I run back
to elsewhere.

Restlessness

My thoughts pace the room.
Bare feet on splintered floors,
looking for a door
that isn't there.

Still, somewhere inside me,
a quiet voice hums.
Not peace yet,
but the promise of it.

Passenger Seat

he pulled up

old Expedition
leather seats
that cracked
when the sun touched them

bass buzzing
door creaked when i climbed in
but i didn't mind
it wasn't the sound
that scared me

not like raised voices
not like voices that
carried heat
even when they laughed

i flinched anyway
kept my eyes down
my shoulders high
like shields

he didn't ask
what i was afraid of
he just

let it be quiet

we ate fries
and listened to music
and nothing hurt
and that was enough

he never raised his voice
never filled the space
with tension

just let me breathe
without bracing

in that seat
beside him
i learned
that safe
doesn't have to come
with silence
and love
doesn't have to come
with fear

Kingdom

The woods were never just woods.
They were a world,
built from bark and breath,
where every leaf whispered
a secret,
and the wind knew my name.

A small creek ran through it,
barely ankle deep,
but to me,
it was an ocean.
I sailed leaves like ships,
fought off pirates with sticks,
and built bridges from stones
that always slipped
just a little.

Tree branches were swords
in my hand,
and I swung them like
the fate of the world
depended on it.

Animals watched from the brush,
not beasts,
but allies.

The fox was a scout.
The crow, my lookout.
Even the ants
were soldiers
marching beneath my rule.

I stayed out too long,
every time.
Sun sinking through the canopy,
painting gold on the dirt path home.
But I was never lost,
just busy
ruling a kingdom
only I could see.

Shape of Me

I am done sanding my edges
to fit into other people's palms.
Let me be rough, honest,
the way wind shapes stone.

I only want to be seen
without shrinking,
loved the way sunlight
loves everything it touches

Light at the End of a Tunnel

It was nothing, really.
A moment small enough to miss,
but it stayed.

Something in the air shifted,
like warmth where there shouldn't be any,
like a soft note in a silent room.

I felt seen,
not in the way of eyes meeting,
but in the way light finds dust,
gently, without meaning to.

And for a heartbeat,
the world wasn't cruel or heavy.
It was just there.
Quiet, kind,
and full of possibility.

VERDANT CANOPY

The Way of the Cat

Cats live as if the world belongs to them—and maybe it does. They move through rooms like royalty, each step deliberate, silent, and certain. You don't own a cat; you coexist with one, orbiting their quiet confidence. They teach you that affection is a privilege, not a guarantee, and when they finally choose to curl into your lap, it feels like a gift from a tiny god.

There's something otherworldly about the way cats carry themselves. Their eyes hold ancient knowing, their stillness a kind of meditation. They are both predator and poet, stretching in sunbeams as if light itself were made for them. They find beauty in small places: a patch of warmth on the floor, the rustle of a paper bag, the dance of dust in a window's glow.

Cats don't hurry, and they don't explain themselves. They remind us that it's okay to take our time, to rest unapologetically, to watch instead of rush. They live entirely on their own terms. Eating when they wish, sleeping where they please, and deciding when you are worthy of their company. Their independence isn't cold; it's honest. They give what they mean and mean what they give.

Sometimes I think cats are reminders of how life could be if we stopped trying so hard—if we trusted our instincts, followed the sun, and didn't apologize for wanting space.

Finding My Way Back Home

When he met me,
I was all edges and echoes
trying to piece together a heart
that had been cracked by too many disappointments.
He didn't rush to fix me.
He just stayed,
quietly holding space for the parts of me
that still trembled when touched.

Then came the days when the world tilted.
When sleepless nights turned into months,
and my reflection felt like a stranger.
Postpartum tears,
the kind that sting without sound.
He sat beside me,
rocking the baby with one arm,
holding me with the other,
as if love could keep us both afloat.

There were panic attacks in grocery stores,
stress from papers that felt heavier than grief,
and mornings when I swore I couldn't do it again.
He became my anchor.
Steady in the storm,
reminding me that even breaking
was a form of becoming.

And then one day,
as I stood in front of my classmates,
capstone nerves running wild through my veins,
I looked up—
and there he was.
California still on his clothes,
a grin soft as sunrise.
He had flown across the miles
just to remind me:
You did it. You always could.

Through heartbreak and healing,
through the ache of growing into myself,
he never flinched.
He saw me.
The me that even I had forgotten.
And in that seeing,
I found my way back home.

One Day

One day,
the lines will come.
They'll map the corners of our laughter,
the nights we stayed up talking
when the world felt too heavy to sleep.

Our hair will gray,
soft silver threads woven through the story of us.
A story built from small, steady moments:
shared coffee, tired smiles,
tiny hands reaching for ours,
the kind of chaos that somehow means joy.

We'll look around this home we built,
and see our love in everything.
In the marks on the walls,
in the worn-out couch where we once held our newborn,
in the garden that grew wild
because we were too busy living.

And I'll still love you the way I do now.
Quietly, endlessly,
in every breath between heartbeats.
You have made this life
something worth growing old in.

If heaven is real,
I think it must feel like this:
your hand in mine,
a house full of laughter,
and the soft knowing
that love like ours
never ends.

We Built a Home from Laughter

We didn't need blueprints.
Just mornings that begin with laughter,
nights that end in shared quiet.

Our walls are made of jokes that never get old,
sounds of joy bouncing down the hallway.
The floors remember our footsteps,
how we danced barefoot in the kitchen
just because the song felt too good to waste.

There's love in the corners,
in the way we pass each other
and still reach out to touch,
in the sound of our son's laughter
echoing off the walls.

This isn't the kind of home
you can buy or build with your hands.
It's the kind that grows,
layer by layer,
every time we choose joy
over silence,
and each other
over everything else.

Becoming the Sunlight

I am not waiting for the light anymore.
I am the light.
I rise without asking permission,
spill warmth across everything I touch.
I've learned that shining isn't arrogance.
It's survival.
The world tried to dim me,
but I grew brighter instead.
A steady blaze, golden and sure,
filling every corner
that once felt cold.
I am not small.
I am not afraid.
I am the sunlight,
and I am finally home in my own glow.

The Library is a Train Station

A library is not a quiet building filled with books. It's a station for the soul. Every shelf hums with the energy of departure, every spine a ticket to somewhere else. The air itself feels alive, heavy with possibility. You step inside, and suddenly you are standing in a station between worlds, the scent of paper and ink like the smell of rain before a long journey.

Each book is a waiting train, its destination unknown until you open the cover. Some will take you through centuries. Others will carry you into someone's memory, or a world that never existed except in the spaces between words. There are no limits here, no borders, no passports required, only curiosity.

You can sit down in the corner of a library and travel farther than any plane could ever take you. The quiet is deceiving. Beneath it, a thousand voices whisper, calling your name. Some tell stories of love and loss, others of war and wonder. Some are so small they could fit in your pocket, and yet when you read them, the universe seems to expand.

The library is where time folds. You might begin your morning in the twenty-first century and find yourself, by afternoon, walking beside a poet in ancient Greece, or listening to the confessions of a queen long forgotten. It's a place where the living and the dead coexist. Authors long gone still speaking, their voices immortal in ink.

There's a strange kind of magic here. You arrive seeking knowledge, but you leave changed. Books don't just teach you things, they re-arrange the furniture of your mind. They remind you that you've been many people before this one, and you will become many more.

Sometimes, when I walk through the aisles, I imagine the books shifting slightly, like trains adjusting on their tracks, preparing for the next traveler. Each title glows faintly, calling out to someone, not everyone, just the one person who needs it most.

And when you finally choose one, it feels like fate, as if the story has been waiting for you all along, patient and sure that you would one day find your way to it.

That's the beauty of libraries: you never quite arrive, and you never really leave. You simply step onto another platform, another story, another life. The trains never stop coming. The journeys never end.

A Warrior's Redemption

You were born into the smoke of broken things.
The kind of life that teaches a boy to run
before he ever learns to pray.
You learned early how to hide your pain
behind a steady hand,
a line of powder,
a laugh that never quite reached your eyes.

The streets became your gospel,
your sermons written in survival.
And when the law came calling,
it wasn't judgment that found you—
it was the gravity of your own past.
Prison walls swallowed you whole,
a steel cathedral where mercy was scarce.

It must have felt like a warzone.
Every corner humming with threat,
every breath measured, cautious.
Concrete floors turned to battlegrounds,
Where trust was a wound you couldn't risk reopening.
Faith flickered like a match in the wind,
but somehow, you kept it lit.

Somewhere in that endless gray,
a crack of light slipped through.

Not salvation in thunder or fire,
but a whisper.
A name you had long ignored
calling you back from the brink.

Now you live quietly,
your hands no longer trembling from sin
but steady in worship.
You rise with the sun,
the same man who once fell into every shadow.
You speak of Jesus like an old friend.
The kind who waited in the wreckage
and never left.

And I, who watched your undoing,
now watch your becoming.
You, who once walked through hell,
now kneel in grace.
Every scar a psalm,
every breath a hymn.

You are proof
that even the lost can come home,
that even the fallen
can fall to their knees
and find Heaven.

Maybe This is Life

The morning is still waking. I sit on the back porch, coffee warm between my hands, watching the sky blush into day. The river shines in the distance, boats cutting through fog, their engines low and steady, like a heartbeat I can almost match my breath to. Birds chatter in the trees, each note a small defiance against silence. The air smells of damp earth and something sweet. Honeysuckle, maybe, or the memory of rain.

I don't move much. The world does it for me. A squirrel scampers along the fence, a leaf drifts onto the patio, the sun slips through branches like it's choosing me on purpose. For once, I don't question it. I just sit here, letting the morning unfold around me, quiet but alive. And I think to myself: maybe this is life. The low hum of boats on the river, the clink of my coffee cup, the music of the birds, the whisper of a new day beginning.

Home Away from Home

The sand here is so white it blinds us,
like snow under a southern sun.
We squint through the shimmer,
our footprints soft as breath in powder.

The waves hush and crash in rhythm,
like the ocean's heartbeat beneath our feet—
steady, familiar, endless.
They carry our laughter,
our arguments, our quiet mornings
spent watching the horizon unfold.

We wake early, before the world stirs,
to search for seashells scattered
like tiny gifts the tide forgot to hide.
The air still smells of night,
and the gulls cry out as if to say:
You're here, again.

By evening, the sky bruises purple and gold.
We chase sand crabs by flashlight,
our laughter echoing against the dark surf,
bare feet kicking up cool drifts of sand.
The sea glows silver in the moonlight,
each wave a whispered secret between us.

We've spent nearly every holiday here:
Christmas presents wrapped in sea breeze,
Fourth of July fireworks stitched
into the Gulf's quiet skin.
Easter spent hunting eggs
in the lobby of the condo,
our laughter rising up the stairwell
like sunlight through the glass door.

The locals wave from porches and shops,
faces we've come to know like old friends.
Our favorite ice cream shop still stands,
and the souvenir shop still hums
with the scent of salt and sunscreen.

This place remembers us.
It folds us in with every return—
as if the sea itself whispers
You're home now.

The Best Ever

They tease me for saying it too much.
This is the best ice cream I've ever had,
This is the best sunset I've ever seen,
This is the best song ever written,
This is the best day of my life.

But I can't help it.
Every small thing feels enormous to me,
every flicker of joy a wildfire in my chest.
This is the best morning I've ever woken to,
the sky soft and unsure of itself,
the coffee too hot, but perfect anyway.

This is the best rain I've ever stood in,
the kind that smells like clean slates and green things.
This is the best breeze,
warm enough to forgive the world
for whatever it did yesterday.

This is the best conversation I've ever had,
words overlapping like waves
rushing to meet the shore.
They roll their eyes,
say I fall in love with everything.
And they're right.
I do.

Because every moment asks to be adored,
and who am I to say no?
The truth is, I don't want to live half-awake,
saving my awe for the extraordinary.
I want to love the cheap candles,
the roadside diners,
the songs that play by accident and feel like fate.

I want to say this is the best
and mean it,

because it is

What the Tree Knows

The tree does not rush its growing.
It bends with the wind,
lets the storm speak,
then stands taller when it passes.
It knows the strength in stillness,
the wisdom in waiting.

It does not beg the sun for warmth.
It trusts the light will return.
It does not envy the flowers.
It knows beauty comes and goes
and still it remains, rooted,
whole within itself.

The tree does not fear change.
It lets go when it must,
and when the time is right,
it begins again.
Quietly, naturally,
without apology.

FALLING LEAVES

rage room

the room hums with silence
before the storm I bring.
i grip the bat like a confession
and the first swing
isn't about the glass
it's about the years
that went unheard.

plates explode like secrets
no one let me speak,
ceramics scream for me,
splinters of memory
raining down
in porcelain prayer.

i don't cry.
i heave.
i rage through it—
grunting, gasping,
as the world
falls apart
in all the right ways.

bottles burst like lungs
finally exhaling,
mirrors crack like truth

i've spent a lifetime
trying not to look at.

no one tells you
how holy it feels
to destroy
what was never yours to carry.

by the end,
i am shaking,
sweating,
spent,
but lighter,
like maybe
this is how
healing begins.

The Walk

The path is soft beneath my feet,
dirt and leaves giving way
like the forest knows
how to hold me.

The trees aren't just trees
they breathe.
Their arms stretch wide overhead,
threading sunlight through green fingers,
casting lace shadows on the ground.

The river appears
sudden and sure.
Not loud,
but endless.
It sparkles like broken glass
tumbling over smooth stones,
singing in a language
I don't speak
but somehow understand.

I crouch near the bank,
let cold water run over my hands
until I forget
what I was holding.

Birdsong echoes
between branches.
The wind tugs gently at my sleeves.
I feel small
in the best kind of way.

There is no schedule here,
no mirrors,
no voices louder than the trees.
Only light,
and breath,
and the hum
of being alive.

And for a while,
I don't carry anything
but my own body.
And that is

enough.

Tiny Heartbeat

I didn't know healing
could have a heartbeat,
could laugh in his sleep,
could tug at my hand
and call me Mom.

My pain used to be a language
I spoke too fluently.
The echo of old wounds,
the weight of what I thought
I'd never outgrow.

But then came you,
small and sure as sunrise,
your joy unafraid of my shadows.
You taught me that broken things
can still glow,
that love doesn't erase the ache,
it grows around it,
like ivy softening a crumbling wall.

Now, when you smile,
I see the proof,
some of the best things
take root in what was once
bare ground.

And maybe healing
isn't the absence of hurt,
but the presence of something
worth staying for.

Standing in the Sunset

The sun sighs low,
spilling orange across the fields,
like a secret told too gently
to be believed.

Pink laces the horizon.
Not loud, not bold,
just a quiet blush
like someone remembering love
from a long time ago.

Clouds stretch like ribbon,
draped in warm fire,
edges soft as breath
on skin.

The world holds its breath—
not in fear,
but in awe,
as day exhales
its final light.

And I stand in it,
painted gold and rose,
feeling small,
but somehow

found.

Letting Go

I loosened my grip
on what once hurt—
and it drifted away
like ash in rain.

Now even the silence
feels lighter.

The Sun I Carry

Once,
I buried myself
beneath everyone else.
A seed forgotten,
pressed deep
in the dark
of wanting to be loved
the right way.

I let the world
walk across my chest
like soil,
believing maybe
If I stayed quiet enough,
still enough,
I'd bloom
into something
beautiful
for them.

But seasons change,
even in the soul.
And something inside me
began to stir.
A root twisting,
a whisper rising,

a hunger
not for approval,
but for light.

Cracks formed
in the lies I'd swallowed.
Soft green reached
toward skies
I'd never dared to name.
And I grew.

I grew
without permission.
It hurt.
The breaking,
the shedding,
the unbecoming
of a thousand silent apologies.
But pain
is the first language
of rebirth.

Now,
I carry the sun
in the way I walk.
My no
is a sacred bloom.
My voice,
a wildflower
refusing

to be trimmed.
I am not who I was.
I am who I needed.
And still,

I grow.

Peace

I'm choosing peace,
leaving chaos behind,
casting off burdens
that never belonged to me,
standing firm,
steady, unshaken.

Phoenix Rising

I was flame.
Burning, breaking, falling to ash,
a fierce fire that consumed itself,
scorching every fragile part.

But in the quiet cold of ruin,
when the world thought me finished,
something stirred beneath the embers.
A pulse, a promise, a spark.

Pain was the blaze that broke me down,
the fire that burned away fear,
the heat that melted doubt and sorrow,
shaping new bones beneath old scars.

From ash and loss, I rose,
wings spread wide,
rising not despite the fire,
but because I was forged within it.

I am reborn,
not as the girl who burned,
but the woman who learned
to fly higher
through every flame.

What I Left Behind

I no longer chase what could have been,
the echoes fade like soft rain,
and I keep walking.

I've stopped mistaking holding on for strength,
some things bloom once.
Then let go.

The past still whispers my name,
but I don't turn around,
it no longer hurts.

What I left behind made room for light,
for quiet mornings,
for growing again.

A Letter to My Son

My sweet boy,

There will never be enough words for you. I could write until the end of time, and still language would fall short. You are beyond every adjective, every metaphor, every line of poetry I've ever written. You are what I mean when I say miracle.

Before you, I didn't know that love could feel like this — something so vast it remakes the world. When I look at you, everything slows down. The noise quiets. The air feels softer. The sun shines differently. You are the reason I believe in goodness, in grace, in the quiet holiness of everyday life.

I love being your mom. Those words feel small, but they hold my whole soul. Being your mom means I get to see life through new eyes every day. You remind me that wonder still exists. Like in raindrops on windows, in the rhythm of laughter, in the small victories no one else notices. You notice everything, and in doing so, you teach me how to live more fully, how to pay attention.

You have this light that can't be explained. It's not loud, but it fills the whole room. It's in your curiosity, your gentleness, your way of seeing the world as if it's both brand new and entirely your own. You make me believe that the world can be kind again.

Some days are hard, I won't pretend otherwise. Life gets heavy, and I don't always have the answers. But then you smile, and it's as if the universe exhales. You are my anchor when the days feel uncertain, and my reminder that love is both fragile and unbreakable.

I look at you and see everything good I've ever done reflected back at me. You make all the noise and struggle of life worth it. You've shown me that love doesn't need to be perfect to be infinite.

I hope you grow knowing this:

You are enough. You don't need to become anything more to be worthy of love. You are already everything you need to be.

And no matter how far you go, or who you become, you will always carry my heart with you. Quietly, steadily, like a heartbeat beneath your own.

You are the reason I am who I am today. You gave me purpose, but more than that, you gave me peace. You made me believe in the kind of love that doesn't fade, the kind that changes everything it touches.

When I look at you, I see proof that something divine exists. Something good and pure that decided I was worthy of you. I will spend the rest of my life trying to deserve that gift.

With all my love,

Mom

ACKNOWLEDGEMENTS

To my husband, Zachary: thank you for helping me see the beauty in the tree's cycle and for inspiring the metaphor that holds this book together. Your love and encouragement helped these roots grow.

To my son, Ezra: you are my greatest joy, my reason, my constant reminder of wonder. Thank you for being you, for filling my days with laughter and light.

To my friends and family: your love, your stories, and your support have shaped so many of these pages. You are the quiet inspiration behind every line.

To my friend, Zee Whiting: thank you for listening to my endless ideas, for brainstorming with me, and for always believing in what this could become.

And finally, to myself: thank you for being brave enough to heal, to write, and to share it all.

ABOUT THE AUTHOR

Brooke lives in Scottsboro, Alabama, with her husband, their son, and two cherished cats. Deeply inspired by the natural world and the power of language, she writes poetry that captures the beauty found in everyday moments and the emotional landscapes of the human experience. Her work reflects a profound appreciation for nature, personal growth, and the quiet transformations that shape our lives. When she is not reading, exploring the outdoors, or collecting inspiration from the world around her, she is crafting poems that invite readers to pause, reflect, and rediscover meaning in their own stories.